KOTOR TRAVEL 2024

CW00481161

(Standard Color Book)

Unlock the Mysteries of Kotor: Your Essential Guide to Exotic
Adventures and Hidden Gems in 2024 and beyond

Kian Wright

DISCLAIMER

Disclaimer

The information contained in this book is for general information purposes only.
The information is provided by the author and while we endeavor to keep the information up to date and correct, we make no representations or warranties of any kind, express or implied, about the completeness, accuracy, reliability, suitability, or availability concerning the book or the information, products, services, or related graphics contained in the book for any purpose. Any reliance you place on such information is therefore strictly at your own risk. In no event will the author or publisher be liable for any loss or damage including without limitation,

indirect or consequential loss or damage, or any loss or damage whatsoever arising from loss of data or profits arising out of, or in connection with, the use of this Book.
Please note that this disclaimer is subject to change without notice.

TABLE OF CONTENT

Introduction to Kotor: A Brief History and Overview

Welcome to Kotor, a mesmerizing fusion of culture, history, and scenic beauty tucked away along Montenegro's stunning Adriatic coast. Let us serve as your guide as you go around this enchanted location, revealing the rich history and contemporary fabric of Kotor.

History of Kotor:

The history of Kotor is both rich and varied. Founded in the second century BC by the Romans, the city has seen several conquests, occupations, and cultural exchanges throughout the ages, leaving a legacy evident in its historic buildings, meandering lanes, and defended walls. Kotor's history, spanning from Byzantine domination to Venetian influence, Ottoman dominance to Austro-Hungarian power, is evidence of the people's flexibility and tenacity.

Kotor Overview:

Respected for its beautifully maintained medieval old town, gorgeous shoreline, and impressive mountain background, Kotor is now recognized as a UNESCO World Heritage Site. Its winding cobblestone alleyways, which are dotted with quaint cafés, upscale stores, and ancient sites at every bend, entice tourists. The striking walls that ring the city provide sweeping views of the blue waters of the Bay of Kotor, which is often called the southernmost fjord in Europe.

What to anticipate in Kotor:

We'll explore the spirit of Kotor on this tour, giving you insider knowledge of its must-see landmarks, undiscovered treasures, delicious food, and outdoor activities. There is something for everyone in Kotor, whether you're an outdoor enthusiast, a history buff, or just looking for a peaceful getaway by the sea.

Kotor Useful Advice:

It's important to acquaint yourself with useful facts before you start your tour, such as local traditions, currencies, and means of transportation. We'll also provide advice on how to get about the busy marketplaces, enjoy real Montenegrin food, and interact with the lively locals.

Accept the Journey in Kotor:

We invite you to savor every second of your trip as you immerse yourself in Kotor's beauty and charm. Discover Kotor via your senses and allow it to make a lasting impression on your spirit, whether you're meandering through historic alleys, sailing around the bay, or taking in a sunset over the Adriatic.

Get ready to go on an incredible journey through the center of Kotor, where modernism meets history and every turn offers a fresh tale just waiting to be explored. Welcome to Kotor, a place where the present is lively, the history is alive, and the future is bright and full of possibilities.

Exploring the Rich History of Kotor:

Explore Kotor's famous sites, such as the Maritime Museum, which provides information on the city's maritime history, and the Cathedral of Saint Tryphon, a 12th-century masterpiece of Romanesque architecture, to learn more about the city's rich past. Explore the old town's maze-like lanes to find secret courtyards and historic churches, or take a leisurely walk around the city walls where history is spoken through every stone.

Accepting Cultural Variations in Kotor:

Kotor's attraction is derived from both its rich cultural scene and historical importance. Visitors are encouraged to fully immerse themselves in the city's cultural fabric, from vibrant festivals honoring cuisine, music, and art to customary performances displaying Montenegrin folklore. Interact with regional craftspeople, savor cuisine from the area, and take part in customs that have been handed down through the ages.

Getting in Touch with Nature in Kotor:

Beyond its charming urban setting, Kotor provides plenty of chances for outdoor enthusiasts to get in touch with the natural world. Put on your hiking boots and climb Mount Lovčen's untamed slopes for expansive views of the sea and the surroundings. Alternatively, go to the calm waters of the Bay of Kotor for a kayaking experience; quiet beaches and undiscovered coves await discovery.

Kotor Sustainability and Conscientious Travel:

It is our responsibility as responsible tourists to take into account how our activities affect the destinations we visit. To protect the city's natural and cultural legacy for future generations, Kotor encourages sustainable tourist activities. Every little deed, from promoting regional companies to reducing plastic waste and honoring regional traditions, helps to keep Kotor's genuineness and allure intact.

We cordially encourage you to embrace the spirit of wonder, adventure, and curiosity that characterizes Kotor as you set out on your trip. Kotor offers an experience that will stick in your mind long after you leave, whether you are attracted to it by its picturesque scenery, rich history, or friendly people. So gather your belongings, let Kotor enchant you, and keep an open mind to new adventures. A thrilling journey is ahead!

Getting Started: Essential Travel Tips and Preparations

Organizing Your Kotor Trip:
Visa Requirements: Nationals of several nations are granted visa-free entry into Montenegro for stays up to ninety days. Before you book your travel, it is important to confirm the visa requirements specific to your country of citizenship. For the most recent information, visit the official Montenegrin government website or get in touch with the closest embassy or consulate.

Select the Best Time to Go: Although summer (June to August) is Kotor's busiest travel period, it also brings with it more crowds and higher costs. Take into account going in the spring or fall, when there are fewer tourists, nicer weather, and more reasonably priced lodging.

Pack Appropriately: Kotor has warm summers and moderate winters. If you want to spend time at the beaches, bring swimsuits and other light, breathable summer gear. Pack extra clothes in the spring and fall for the chilly nights. When touring the city's cobblestone streets, don't forget to pack necessities like comfortable walking shoes, a hat, sunglasses, and sunscreen.

How to Travel to Kotor
By Air:

The main international airport serving Montenegro is **Podgorica Airport** (TGD), which is situated around 90 kilometers north of Kotor. Major European cities are served by flights operated by airlines such as Montenegro Airlines and other European carriers.

Tivat Airport (TIV): Offering more convenience for passengers, Tivat Airport is just 10 kilometers from Kotor. Several European airlines service it, including low-cost carriers like Ryanair in the summer.

By Land:

Bus: Kotor has excellent bus connections to nearby cities and nations. Major cities such as Belgrade (Serbia), Tirana (Albania), and Dubrovnik (Croatia) have regular services. Kotor's major bus terminal is conveniently situated in the city center.

Car: The road system in Montenegro is well-maintained, and driving provides freedom if that's your preference. Though there are beautiful views from the coastal route, be ready for twisty roads and rugged terrain. You may rent a vehicle online ahead of time, in major cities, and at airports.

By Water:

Cruise Ships: Throughout the Adriatic, cruise ships often stop in Kotor. At the harbor, which is situated just outside of the old town, cruise guests disembark. The city center is just a short stroll away from there.

How to Navigate Kotor:

Walking: Because of its small streets and pedestrian-only areas, Kotor's ancient town is best explored on foot. The majority of the main sights, eateries, and retail establishments are all easily accessible by foot.

Public Transportation: Although Kotor is small and easily navigable on foot, there are public buses that go to other towns and tourist destinations. Routes to Budva, Perast, and other locations around the Bay of Kotor are offered by the city's major bus terminal.

Taxi and ridesharing: In Kotor, taxis are easily found and may be booked via smartphone applications or by hailing one on the street. In some places, ridesharing services like Uber are also available.

Boat Tours: You might think about going on a boat trip to explore the bay and see neighboring islands like Saint George and Our Lady of the Rocks. Numerous regional businesses provide guided tours that leave from Kotor's shoreline.

Kotor Crucial Details:

Currency: The official currency of Montenegro is the euro (EUR). Kotor has plenty of ATMs, and the majority of lodging facilities, eateries, and retail establishments take credit cards. But, it's a good idea to have some cash on hand for little transactions and unexpected expenses.

Language: Although English is commonly used, particularly in tourist areas, Montenegrin is the official language. Knowing a few simple words in Montenegrin might help you communicate with people and appreciate their culture.

Safety: Although Kotor is typically safe for tourists, it's important to exercise caution, particularly at night and in busy locations. After dusk, stay away from remote locations, guard your possessions, and exercise caution against small-time theft.

Healthcare: Kotor has access to pharmacies and medical facilities, and Montenegro has a respectable healthcare system. Having travel insurance that pays for medical costs, including emergency evacuation if necessary, is advised.

With this thorough planning and travel advice, you'll be ready to go to Kotor with confidence. Kotor's charm and beauty await you whether you arrive by air, land, or sea and whether you want to explore the city on foot, by public transit, or by boat. Get ready for an amazing journey in this charming and historic location on Montenegro's Adriatic coast. Happy travels!

Montenegro's road and driving conditions:

If you are traveling from Bosnia-Herzegovina, you will mostly be traveling on one-lane country roads.

It may be challenging to pass on a single-lane road in such hazardous circumstances since you will be traveling alone. Never attempt to pass someone unless you have a good vision!

Plan for extra driving time since you'll be passing through tiny towns most of the time and the typical speed limit on one-lane roads is around 50 km/h.

Avoid speeding! Every few kilometers, one could see the Montenegrin Police Force aggressively stopping vehicles for various offenses, including speeding.

The fact that street lights flash green before turning red does not always indicate you have plenty of time to pass through the light!

There is no interior framework, no lighting, and no ventilation in tunnels. Activate your lights!

When driving, be prepared for potholes, which occur often. Also, drive gently! The last thing you want is for it to burst a tire in a remote location with no one around to assist!

Always give it your all! There are many petrol stations in coastal cities, but it will be more difficult to find them in the highlands and smaller communities.

When you get anywhere in Montenegro, use a GPS navigation system, but be sure you stick to the major highways! However, we purchased a map book of Europe just in case, as many routes have not yet been plotted out.

In low season, crossing the border from Bosnia into Montenegro might take between thirty and one hour. I can see how lines would become longer after May.

You have to provide your passports, auto insurance documents, and vehicle registration! Consult your automobile rental business if you're renting a vehicle.

For the duration of the road journey, it is also advised to have an international driver's license, however, it is not required (except for Albania and Kosovo).

If you're planning to travel from Montenegro to Macedonia, avoid using that route. Rather, you'll have to take Lac by car across Albania. Here, you will undoubtedly need to provide your foreign driver's license.

Cows and other cattle are often seen strolling down the road. Avoid racing around turns since anything can be just around the corner.

Remain on all primary routes! Never stray from the road's edge or onto unpaved trails.

Watch out for neighborhood farmers who may be operating donkey or horse-drawn buggies on the road. They don't move very quickly for obvious reasons, so don't pass them until you have a clear way!

At the first (unsafe) opportunity, Montenegrins tend to tailgate and overtake, which puts you and them in danger of almost causing an accident. Remain calm and allow them to go.

Outdoor Adventures: Hiking, Cycling, and Water Sports in Kotor

The breathtaking natural scenery of Kotor is the ideal setting for a variety of outdoor activities, including exciting water sports, peaceful bike rides, and strenuous treks. Kotor has something to offer any outdoor enthusiast, whether they're searching for heart-pounding sports or just want to take in the beauty of the natural world.

Hiking:
1. Vrmac Ridge Trail

Address: Jadranska magistrala, Bogdašići, Montenegro

- **Guided tour:** Join knowledgeable local guides for a guided trek along the picturesque Vrmac Ridge Trail. The trip usually begins close to Kotor's old town and travels through verdant woods and historical locations, providing sweeping views of the Bay of Kotor as it goes. For visitors of all ability levels, guides provide insights into the history, ecology, and wildlife of the region, resulting in an unforgettable and instructive experience.
- **Time:** Around four to five hours.
- The track is appropriate for those with a moderate degree of fitness, however, it does include some steep and rough portions.

2. Lovćen National Park:

Address: Cetinje, Montenegro
Phone: +382 67 863 214

- Take a guided tour to the peak of Mount Lovćen in Lovćen National Park, lasting a whole day. Participants set out on a demanding but rewarding adventure through a variety of environments, including thick woods, mountainous hills, and alpine meadows, under the guidance of professional guides.
- Discover the park's rich biological variety and cultural value as you go, and take in expansive vistas of the sea and neighboring mountains.
- The tour will run for six to eight hours.
- There are difficult parts of the climb to Mount Lovčen, therefore physical fitness is a must.

3. Mountain Orjen:

- **Tour with a guide:** Take an exciting all-day climb with a guide to the top of Mount Orjen, which is situated where Bosnia and Herzegovina and Montenegro meet. Participants go over steep slopes, alpine meadows, and rough terrain under the guidance of knowledgeable guides while taking in breath-blowing views of the Adriatic shoreline and the surrounding areas. For experienced hikers looking for an exhilarating outdoor experience, this strenuous journey offers a spectacular outdoor adventure.
- The tour lasts for a whole day, perhaps seven or eight hours.
- A challenging task. The trip to Mount Orjen is appropriate for experienced hikers with a high degree of fitness since it includes rocky terrain, steep ascent,s, and descents.

Cycling:
1. Bay of Kotor Cycling Route:

- **Guided trip:** Take a guided bicycle trip around the coastal roads to see the charming Bay of Kotor. Participants cycle through quaint towns, famous sites, and breathtaking vistas while being led by experts who impart knowledge of the history and culture of the area. This easy ride, appropriate for all skill levels, provides breathtaking vistas of the bay and plenty of chances for picture ops along the route.
- There are alternatives for a half-day or full-day duration.
- Moderately easy to difficult. The cycling path is appropriate for riders of all ages and skill levels since it is mostly level with a few short, mild hills.

2. Lustica Peninsula:

- **Guided trip:** Join experienced local guides for a guided cycling trip to see the Lustica Peninsula's natural beauty. While learning about the history and culture of the region, participants bike through traditional towns, vineyards, and olive groves, fully immersing themselves in the Mediterranean beauty. This trip, which is appropriate for cyclists with some experience, includes a combination of paved and off-road paths and allows riders to modify their itineraries to suit their tastes.
- There are alternatives for a half-day or full-day duration.
- Moderate in difficulty. riding enthusiasts with a modest degree of fitness and basic riding abilities may enjoy the brief hills and off-road areas of the Lustica Peninsula's bike trails.

3. Mountain biking:

For bike renting contact:
MonteBicycle Bike Rental & Servicing
Address: Karla Radoničića, Kotor 85331, Montenegro
Phone: +382 69 221 023

- **Guided Tour:** Take a guided tour across the harsh terrain of Kotor to start an exciting mountain riding journey. Participants explore difficult terrain, steep slopes, and forest paths under the guidance of knowledgeable guides while taking in breath-blowing vistas of the bay and neighboring mountains. This route, which is appropriate for experienced mountain bikers, provides heart-pounding descents and challenging terrain for a memorable outdoor experience.
- There are alternatives for a half-day or full-day duration.
- Kotor's mountain bike routes are best suited for those with prior mountain riding expertise and a high degree of fitness since they may include steep descents, rocky portions, and tricky difficulties.

Water Activities:

1. Stand-up paddleboarding and kayaking:

Kayak Tours Kotor
Plaza Urc, Kotor 85550, Montenegro
+382 67 085 865

- **Guided Tour:** Experience the splendor of the Bay of Kotor with a tour leader who specializes in stand-up paddleboarding or kayaking. Paddle across pristine seas to discover isolated beaches, sea caves, and secret coves while taking in breathtaking views of the surrounding terrain. This journey provides a unique viewpoint of Kotor's coastline and marine life, making it appropriate for both novice and expert paddlers.
- Time: two to four hours.
- Accredited guides will give guidance to participants of all ability levels.

2. Boat and Sailing Tours:

A Day Out on Yacht Monty B
Put I Bokeljski Brigade Dobrota Kotor, 85331, Montenegro
+382 67 859 309

- **Guided excursion:** Take a sailing or boat excursion with knowledgeable captains and guides to see the wonders of the Bay of Kotor. While taking in the stunning views, historic sites, and quaint towns along the coast, participants may also learn about the history and culture of the area. This excursion, which is appropriate for small parties, families, and couples, provides leisure, discovery, and excitement on the water.
- There are alternatives for a half-day or full-day duration.
- Easy in terms of difficulty. Offers swimming, snorkeling, and sunbathing possibilities for individuals of all ages and skill levels.

3. kitesurfing or windsurfing:

Kiteloop - Kitesurfing and Wing foil lessons in Montenegro
Velika Plaza, 85360, Montenegro
+381 64 1729033

- **Guided trip:** Take a windsurfing or kitesurfing trip with knowledgeable instructors and ride the waves of the Bay of Kotor. By using the wind to their advantage, participants may glide over the water and execute thrilling maneuvers while taking in expansive views of the bay and the surrounding countryside. This trip provides thrills and heart-pounding excitement for those who like water activities and is appropriate for riders who are intermediate to advanced.
- Time: two to three hours.
- Moderate to advanced in difficulty. It is recommended that participants possess prior windsurfing or kitesurfing expertise and exhibit comfort in a range of wind and sea conditions.

Tips for Guided Tour:
- **Make Your Reservations in Advance:** Especially during the busiest times the of year, guided excursions often sell out. It is advised that you

reserve your trip in advance, either online or via a local tour operator, to guarantee your position.

- **Verify Inclusions:** Pay close attention to the list of included services before reserving a guided tour. Transportation, equipment rentals, training, refreshments, and any required admission fees could all fall under this category.
- **Pay Close Attention to Instructions:** Pay close attention to the advice given by your guides, particularly to safety precautions and appropriate techniques. You and the other participants will have a safe and pleasurable experience as a result of this.
- **Respect the Environment:** Travel responsibly by showing consideration for the surrounding ecosystem and any places of cultural significance that you visit. Refrain from disturbing animals, remain on authorized routes, and do not litter.
- **Maintain Hydration and Sun Protection:** Engaging in outdoor activities, particularly during warm weather, maybe physically taxing. To shield your skin from the sun's rays, don't forget to use sunscreen often and remain hydrated by drinking plenty of water.
- **Enjoy Yourself:** Above all, relax and enjoy the moment! Soak in the sights, sounds, and feelings of Kotor's outdoor treasures; guided excursions are meant to provide a delightful and unforgettable encounter.

You're ready to go on a guided outdoor adventure in Kotor if you keep these pointers in mind, whether you're trekking through picturesque scenery, riding along the coast, or exploring the bay's pristine waters. So gather your belongings, put on your shoes, and get ready for an incredible adventure in one of the most stunning locations in Montenegro!

Accommodation Options: Where to Stay in Kotor for Every Budget

Kotor has a wide range of lodging choices to fit any traveler's taste and budget, from opulent hotels to quaint guesthouses and affordable hostels.

These three categories of lodging are listed with illustrations of each:

1. Luxury Hotels

a. Hotel Forza Mare:

b.b. 85 330 bb, Kriva, Dobrota 85331, Montenegro
+382 32 333 500
$231 per Night

- Offering opulent lodging with breathtaking views of the sea, Hotel Forza Mare is situated near the waterfront. Featuring exquisite decor and contemporary conveniences, guests may enjoy large rooms and suites. The hotel has a gourmet restaurant, a private beach area, indoor and outdoor pools, and a spa on site.
- Hotel Forza Mare visitors get attentive attention, a free breakfast, and access to exclusive areas like the beach club and health center. The hotel's ideal location makes it simple to see Kotor's attractions, and its calm ambiance makes it a tranquil place to unwind.

b. Palazzo Radomiri Hotel:

bb Kriva, Dobrota 85331, Montenegro
+382 69 214 123
$219 Per Night

- The Palazzo Radomiri Hotel provides a unique combination of contemporary elegance and historic charm, all housed in a tastefully refurbished 18th-century palace. Antique furniture and modern conveniences combine to create a distinctive design in each room and suite. In addition to enjoying magnificent views from the terrace and

Mediterranean food at the on-site restaurant, guests may unwind in the hotel's garden courtyard.

- The Palazzo Radomiri Hotel offers individualized service and a calm setting, making it a peaceful haven from Kotor's busy streets. Despite being close to the old town and waterfront promenade by foot, guests may relax in the hotel's cozy environment, which is surrounded by verdant gardens and ancient buildings.

c. Hotel Casa del Mare - Amfora:

Orahovac bb, Kotor 85330, Montenegro
+382 32 305 852

- The Hotel Casa del Mare - Amfora is a magnificent beachfront hideaway with stunning views of the bay, tucked away in the charming hamlet of Dobrota. The hotel has a health center, gourmet restaurant, rooftop infinity pool, and tastefully furnished rooms and suites. Direct access to the beach and free kayak and paddleboard rentals are additional benefits for visitors.
- With individualized service and high-end facilities, Hotel Casa del Mare-Amfora offers a unique environment for rest and renewal. During their visit, guests may fully immerse themselves in luxury and comfort, whether they want to explore the gorgeous surroundings, indulge in spa treatments, or just relax by the pool.

2. Boutique Guesthouses:
a. Villa Ivana:

Kotor Vista, 265, Montenegro
- Located in the center of Kotor's ancient town, Villa Ivana provides quaint boutique lodging in a

historically significant environment. The guesthouse offers comfortable rooms and suites that are individually designed with both classic and contemporary furniture. Free breakfast is available in the courtyard area for visitors, along with customized tour suggestions.

- With friendly hospitality and attentive service, Villa Ivana offers a genuine Montenegrin experience. Indulge in Kotor's rich history and culture while relaxing in the cozy confines of a boutique guesthouse right in the heart of the city.

b. Hotel Hippocampus:

Kotor 489, Kotor 85330, Montenegro
+382 67 149 448
$137 Per Night

- Hotel Hippocampus is housed in a painstakingly renovated 17th-century edifice that combines classic beauty with modern sophistication. The boutique hotel provides tastefully furnished rooms and suites with contemporary conveniences mixed with old wooden beams and stone walls. Visitors may unwind on the rooftop terrace of the hotel, take in the expansive views of the bay, and eat at the on-site restaurant that serves regional specialties.

- Located in the center of Kotor's UNESCO-listed ancient town, Hotel Hippocampus provides a distinctive fusion of luxury and history, making for an unforgettable stay for visitors. The hotel's cozy setting and attentive service guarantee a pleasant and unforgettable stay, and its handy location makes it simple to see the city's attractions.

v. Hotel Villa Duomo:

Stari grad 358, Kotor 85330, Montenegro
+382 32 323 111
$122 Per Night

- Situated in a peaceful area of the historic district, Hotel Villa Duomo provides upscale lodging inside a meticulously renovated 18th-century edifice. The hotel offers tastefully decorated rooms and suites, each with a distinct personality and charm. The hotel offers free breakfast, a courtyard area for guests to

27

relax in, and concierge services tailored to their needs.

- With individualized care and meticulous attention to detail, Hotel Villa Duomo offers a tranquil haven in the center of Kotor. Visitors may unwind in the tranquil settings of the hotel and get away from the bustle of the city, all while being able to stroll to Kotor's major attractions and waterfront promenade.

3. Budget-friendly Hostels:

a. Hostel Old Town Kotor:

Stari Grad 284, Kotor 85339, Montenegro
+382 68 437 471
$42 per Night

- Located in the heart of Kotor's historic district, Old Town Hostel Kotor provides reasonably priced lodging in a handy location. Both private and dorm-style rooms are available at the hostel; all have common restrooms and standard amenities. The communal spaces, which include a rooftop terrace with expansive city views, are ideal for guest interaction.
- Old Town Hostel Kotor offers a cozy and welcoming base for visiting Kotor and its environs for tourists on a tight budget. The hostel's central location makes it simple to see the city's attractions, and its social environment promotes conversation and experience-sharing among guests.

b. Montenegro Hostel Kotor:

Dobrota Donji put bb, Kotor 85330, Montenegro
+382 68 451 431

- Located just outside the old town, the laid-back Montenegro Hostel Kotor provides reasonably priced lodging. The hostel offers individual and dorm-style accommodations with communal restrooms and minimal amenities. In addition to cooking in the shared kitchen, guests may relax in the hostel's courtyard garden and mingle in the common rooms.
- The Montenegro Hostel Kotor offers inexpensive visitors a cozy and unhurried setting for seeing Kotor and its environs. The welcoming personnel at the hostel can suggest places to eat, go, and things to do. They also have extensive local knowledge.

c. Villa Old Mariner:

Prcanj 136, 85330, Montenegro
+382 69 363 777
$51 Per night

- In the center of Kotor's ancient town, the ancient Villa Old Mariner provides affordable lodging in a historic environment. The guesthouse offers both private and dorm-style accommodations, both with basic furniture and communal restrooms. Visitors may unwind on the rooftop terrace with views of the city and enjoy the complimentary breakfast that is offered in the common area.

- Villa Old Mariner offers an affordable, friendly base for seeing Kotor's old town and surrounding areas for visitors on a tight budget. The guesthouse's convenient location makes it simple to reach the city's restaurants, sights, and nightlife, and its welcoming environment and pleasant atmosphere make visitors feel at home away from home. Old Mariner Guesthouse & Hostel is a great option for those on a tight budget who want to take in the beauty and history of Kotor's old town without going overboard because of its reasonable prices and simple facilities.

Kotor offers a variety of lodging alternatives to meet the requirements and tastes of every tourist, including boutique guesthouses with a touch of history, affordable hostels with a lively environment, and luxurious lodgings with individualized service.

Every lodging option, from little guesthouses tucked away in the old town's winding lanes to beachfront hotels giving expansive views of the bay, adds something special to your stay in this alluring coastal location.

During your vacation to Kotor, you may choose the ideal location to call home with a variety of conveniences and privileges available, guaranteeing a pleasant and unforgettable stay from beginning to end.

Kotor Top Attractions and Hidden Gems

Here is a thorough guide to the must-see sights and lesser-known treasures in Kotor for visitors and tourists to explore:

Top Attractions:
1. Kotor Old Town:

Stari Grad 303, Kotor 85330, Montenegro
+382 69 991 962

- Discover the enchanting cobblestone lanes and ancient structures of Kotor's UNESCO-listed old town, which is encircled by medieval walls and watched over by the towering St. John stronghold. Explore architectural wonders like the Maritime Museum, St. Tryphon Cathedral, and lively squares brimming with eateries and retail establishments.

- Highlights include strolling around the city walls, seeing the exquisite stone carvings of the Cathedral of Saint Tryphon, and ascending the 1,350 steps to St. John's Fortress for expansive views of the city and harbor.
- **Advice:** To escape the crowds, visit in the early morning or late afternoon. To get insight into the history and culture of Kotor's old town, enroll in a guided walking tour.

2. Bay of Kotor:

- Experience the breathtaking Bay of Kotor by boat or car; it's often called the southernmost fjord in Europe. Admire the rough mountains, charming towns, and glistening bay waters that are peppered with historic sites and old churches.
- Take a tour of the fortified island of Our Lady of the Rocks, visit the quaint coastal villages of Perast and Herceg Novi, and take in the expansive vistas from the winding Lovćen Mountain route.
- **Advice:** Hire a kayak or paddleboard to explore the bay's coastline's secret beaches and isolated coves.

While there, eat fresh seafood at Perast's waterfront eateries.

3. Lovćen National Park:

- Explore the breathtaking natural splendor of Lovćen National Park, which is home to Mount Lovćen and some of the most breathtaking views in all of Montenegro. Trek over rocky terrain, alpine meadows, and lush woods while taking in breath-blowing vistas of the surrounding Alps and the Adriatic Sea.
- Explore beautiful hiking paths like the Njegošev Put, see the tomb of Petar II Petrović-Njegoš at the top of Mount Lovćen, and take in expansive views from overlooks like Krstac Pass.
- A lot of water and good hiking shoes are recommended since the park's routes may be difficult and steep. Take a trip in the early morning or late afternoon when it's cooler outside and less crowded.

4. Perast:

- Discover the charming town of Perast, renowned for its exquisite views of the sea and well-preserved

Baroque buildings. Admire famous sites like the Church of Our Lady of the Rocks and St. Nicholas Church as you meander through the winding lanes dotted with mansions and churches.

- Highlights include dining at waterfront restaurants serving fresh seafood and regional cuisine, climbing the bell tower of St. Nicholas Church for panoramic views, and taking a boat excursion to Our Lady of the Rocks island.
- **Advice:** To experience Perast's ancient charm, explore it on foot. If possible, arrive in the early morning or late afternoon to avoid crowds.

5. Our Lady of the Rocks

- Discover the distinctive artificial island of Our Lady of the Rocks, situated in the Bay of Kotor. This man-made island is home to a stunning museum and Baroque cathedral that are brimming with religious relics and nautical treasures.

- Explore the museum to learn about the history and customs of the island, take in the breathtaking paintings and frescoes within the church, and relax on the island's terrace to take in the breathtaking views of the bay.
- **Advice:** To get to the island, take a boat excursion from Perast or Kotor. While there, be sure to see neighboring sites like the Blue Cave and Mamula Fortress.

Undiscovered Treasures:
1. St. Nikola Church:

- Located just outside of Kotor's ancient town, St. Nikola Church is a peaceful place to escape the throng. This charming church is a serene haven for anyone looking for seclusion because of its lovely bell tower and breathtaking views of the harbor.
- Highlights include exploring the inside of the church with its elaborate paintings and religious items, climbing the bell tower for sweeping views of Kotor

and the surrounding area, and taking time to sit quietly in the peaceful courtyard.

- **Advice:** Be mindful of the church's religious importance and schedule your visit for the best light and the fewest number of visitors in the morning or late afternoon.

2. Vrmac Ridge

gornja last, Montenegro

- Take a stroll along the Vrmac Ridge to get amazing views of the surrounding mountains and the Bay of Kotor. This picturesque path provides a tranquil haven from the bustle of the city and is great for picnics, birding, and photography.
- Take in expansive views from overlooks along the crest as you follow the well-marked path through verdant trees and rugged terrain. During the spring and summer, keep an eye out for wildlife, including raptors and blooming wildflowers.
- **Advice:** Since there aren't many amenities along the path, wear supportive hiking shoes and pack plenty of water and food. To avoid the heat of the day,

begin your journey early in the morning and be ready for any changes in the weather.

3. Kotorska Scala:

- Explore Kotorska Skala, a quiet beach tucked away in the Bay of Kotor amid towering cliffs, a hidden treasure. This immaculate length of beach is the ideal place for swimming, tanning, and relaxing with its clean seas, golden sands, and breathtaking views of the neighboring mountains.
- Swim in the cool bay waters, spend the day lounging on the beach, and explore the neighboring caves and rock formations. Pack a picnic lunch and have a leisurely meal while taking in the view of the bay, or stop by one of the beach bars for some snacks and drinks.
- **Advice:** Wear sturdy shoes and be ready for a short but strenuous climb since Kotorska Skala can only be reached via a steep and narrow trail. Since the beach might become congested during the busiest travel season, get there early to guarantee a good location.

4. Sveti Đorđe Island:

- Explore Sveti Đorđe Island, a hidden treasure in the Bay of Kotor, which is close to Perast. This deserted island provides peace and unspoiled natural beauty, as well as the historic Benedictine abbey.
- See the island's remote beaches, hiking paths, and ancient ruins via boat trip. Take pleasure in swimming, snorkeling, and having a picnic away from the throng in this beautiful location.
- **Advice:** Take a boat cruise from Perast or Kotor to Sveti Đorđe Island, and carry your food and beverages since the island is undeveloped.

5. Fort Gorazda:

Skaljari, Montenegro

- Wander up to Fort Gorazda, a hidden treasure perched above Kotor's historic district. This old fortification is the ideal location for photography and sunset viewing since it provides expansive views of the city, bay, and neighboring mountains.
- Travel through woodlands and rugged terrain as you hike along the picturesque path from Kotor's ancient town to the fortress. Discover the fortress's remains, then go to the top for vistas that cannot be seen anywhere else.

Advice: Because the terrain may be steep and difficult, use supportive hiking shoes and carry plenty of water. To escape the heat of the day and take advantage of the calmer surroundings, visit in the early morning or late afternoon.

Discover an abundance of captivating coastal destinations, including the pristine vistas of Lovćen National Park, the ancient alleyways of Kotor's old town, and hidden jewels like Kotorska Skala and St. Nikola Church. Kotor has something to offer any kind of tourist, whether they are looking for off-the-beaten-path adventures, scenic natural splendor, or cultural sites. Prepare to be amazed by the beauty and charm of Kotor, Montenegro's undiscovered jewel on the Adriatic coast, by packing your luggage and putting on your shoes.

Kotor has many chances for discovery and adventure because of its fascinating history, breathtaking scenery, and hidden treasures just waiting to be found. You will be enthralled by the beauty and charm of this Adriatic coast jewel whether you are climbing the panoramic views of Fort Gorazda, marveling at the medieval architecture of Perast, or discovering the serene serenity of Sveti Đorđe Island. So gather your spirit of adventure and get ready to explore Kotor's treasures, as there are tales to be told around every corner.

Museums and Galleries in Kotor

1. Maritime Museum of Montenegro:

391 Trg Bokeljskemorrice, Kotor 85330, Montenegro
+382 32 304 720

The Maritime Museum of Montenegro provides insight into the region's rich nautical history and cultural heritage and is situated in the center of Kotor's old town. The museum, housed in the old Grgurina Palace, has an extensive collection of relics, interactive displays, and exhibitions covering centuries of naval conflict, commerce, and marine exploration.

See displays including historical papers, nautical equipment, model ships, and marine relics about Montenegro's maritime heritage. Discover Kotor's history as a key Adriatic commerce center, its maritime regulations, and the influence of naval warfare and piracy on the area.

Travelers have a better knowledge of Montenegro's maritime history and how important it was in forming the region's culture. The museum provides visitors of all ages with educational programs, guided tours, and special events, making it a worthwhile visit for both families and history buffs.

2. Kotor City walla and fortifications:

Explore the historic city walls and defenses of Kotor, a UNESCO World Heritage Site, and take a step back in time. These impressive defense walls, which date back to the Venetian period, ring the old town and provide expansive views of the surrounding mountains, harbor, and city.

Take a stroll around the immaculate city walls, ascend the 1,350 steps to St. John's Fortress, and take in the views of iconic structures like the Sea Gate and Clock Tower. With the help of educational signage and guided tours, discover the history and importance of the city walls.

Tourists learn about the military past, architectural legacy, and strategic significance of Kotor as a fortified Adriatic coast city. The city walls provide a special location for photography, touring, and taking in Kotor's splendor and beauty from above.

3. Boka Navy Museum:

Explore the maritime past of the Bay of Kotor by visiting the Boka Navy Museum, housed in the storied Grgurina Palace in the ancient town of Kotor. This museum highlights the nautical prowess and strategic significance of the Boka Bay area throughout history by showcasing its maritime traditions and accomplishments.

Take a look at exhibits that illustrate the development of shipbuilding, naval technology, and maritime culture in the Bay of Kotor. They include interactive displays, historical documents, and model ships. Discover the major naval conflicts, voyages, and trade routes that influenced the nautical history of the area.

Tourists have a greater understanding of the Boka Navy's role in safeguarding the bay's coastal towns, promoting commerce and cross-cultural interaction, and maintaining Montenegrin maritime customs. The museum provides entertaining and instructive activities, guided tours, and special events for guests of all ages, making it a worthwhile visit for families and history buffs.

4. Kotor Cats Museum:

Trg Gospa od Anđela - Stari Grad 371, Kotor 85330, Montenegro

Explore the amazing world of cats at Kotor's Cats Museum, which honors the furry citizens who have long been cherished figures in the local mythology and culture. This unique museum, which is housed in an ancient stone structure in the old town, provides an entertaining and educational look into the mythology, history, and symbolism surrounding cats in Kotor.

Take in displays showcasing global cat-themed artifacts, writing, artwork, and memorabilia, such as medieval manuscripts, Egyptian cat sculptures, and modern cat-inspired clothing. Via interactive exhibits and multimedia presentations, discover the importance of cats in Kotor's maritime history, superstitions, and everyday life.

Guests leave with a fresh understanding of the importance of cats in Kotor culture and their ongoing appeal as lucky charms, friends, and protectors. For cat enthusiasts of all ages, the museum's colorful displays and playful ambiance make it an enjoyable and memorable visit, complete with picture opportunities and mementos to remember your time there.

5. Palace of Pima:

At the Palace of Pima, a historic palace in the center of Kotor's ancient town, take a step back in time. The collection of artwork, antique furniture, and ornamental arts housed in this graceful palace from the Renaissance period provides insight into the extravagant lifestyle of Kotor's aristocratic families during the Venetian era.

Take in the lavish design of the palace's apartments, which include a dining room, grand salon, and individual rooms with tapestries, frescoes, and antique furnishings. Admire the paintings, sculptures, and ornamental items created by Italian and local artisans that capture the aesthetic and cultural preferences of the upper Renaissance society.

Visitors learn about the patronage of the arts, diplomatic ties, and contributions to the development of the city, as well as the social, cultural, and artistic environment of Kotor's nobility during the Venetian period. For those who are interested in both history and art, the Palace of Pima is a must-visit location since it provides guided tours and cultural activities that provide a greater knowledge of its historical importance and architectural grandeur.

6. St. Luke's Church and Icon Museum:

Trg Sv. Luke, Kotor 85330, Montenegro

Discover Kotor's rich religious history at the Icon Museum and St. Luke's Church, which are situated in the ancient town. A collection of medieval-era Orthodox icons that highlight the creative and spiritual traditions of Montenegro's Orthodox Christian community may be found within this ancient church.

Take in the elaborate iconography and holy craftsmanship of the church's interior, which has icons that represent events from the lives of the Virgin Mary, Jesus, and other saints. Discover the meaning and religious symbolism ingrained in these revered pieces of art as you study the background and importance of icon painting in Montenegrin culture.

Visitors learn about the significance of icons in religious practice, devotion, and worship, as well as the religious and cultural legacy of the Orthodox Christian population in Montenegro. The museum is an invaluable resource for learning about the spiritual traditions of Kotor and the surrounding area since it provides guided tours and educational events that contextualize and explain the symbols on exhibit.

Kotor has something for every interest and curiosity, from modern art and cultural heritage to maritime history and naval traditions, with its wide range of museums and galleries. Visitors to Kotor will undoubtedly be enthralled by the abundance of tales, relics, and artwork on exhibit, whether they want to explore the marine museums of Montenegro, delve into the world of cats at the Cats Museum, or take in the medieval magnificence of the Palace of Pima. Hence, throughout your visit, take your time, get engrossed in the displays, and let the rich tapestry of Kotor's museums and galleries reveal itself to you.

Itinerary options needed to explore Kotor like a local

Here is a suggested schedule with day-by-day tips to help you see Kotor like a local:
Day 1: Visit the Old Town of Kotor
Morning:

- In Kotor's ancient town, begin your day with a leisurely breakfast at a neighborhood café. Savor freshly made coffee with traditional Montenegrin pastries like burek or palatine (crepes).
- Take a self-guided walking tour of Kotor's historic town after breakfast. Explore secret squares and alleys, take in the splendor of ancient buildings, and meander through tiny cobblestone pathways.

Clock Tower
Address: Square of the Arms, Kotor, Montenegro

St. Tryphon Cathedral
- See famous sites including the **Clock Tower** , the **Maritime Museum** , and **St. Tryphon Cathedral** . For sweeping views of the harbor and neighboring mountains, climb the city walls.

In the afternoon:

Konoba Scala Santa restaurant
Address: Trg od Salate, Old Town, Bay of Kotor, 85330, 85330, Montenegro
Phone: +382 67 393 458

- Visit a classic **Konoba Scala Santa (tavern)** or restaurant for lunch to sample regional cuisine like cevapi (grilled sausages), grilled meats, or seafood risotto. Enjoy your meal with a cool local beer or a sip of wine from Montenegro.
- Wander around the crowded market area and look at the vendors offering handmade goods, fresh fruit, and trinkets. Talk to the locals and try some of the specialties from the area, such as cheeses, honey, and olives.

Evening:
- Take a leisurely passeggiata (evening walk) along the waterfront promenade with the locals as the sun sets. Admire the lit old town and observe the fishing boats making their way back to the port.

- Savor supper in a Mediterranean-themed restaurant on the waterfront. Savor delicacies like seafood platters, grilled fish, and octopus salad while taking in the vibrant ambiance.
- Visit one of Kotor's gelaterias or cafés to round off your day with an espresso or gelato. Think back on your exploration-filled day and make plans for tomorrow's excursions.

Day 2: Find Undiscovered Treasures and Regional Favorites

Morning:

- Take a stroll to Fort Gorazda, a hidden treasure that offers sweeping views of the sea and Kotor, to start your day. Bring a picnic basket and have breakfast at the top while admiring the amazing view.
- Make your way down from the citadel and discover Kotor's peaceful districts beyond the ancient town walls. Explore quiet neighborhoods, take in the beauty of old buildings, and find secret gardens and courtyards.

In the afternoon:

- Go to Kotorska Skala, a remote beach tucked away along the bay between rocks. Unwind and swim in this beautiful environment away from the throng throughout the day.
- Bring a picnic for lunch, or stop by a nearby beach bar that serves light fare and cool beverages. As you rejuvenate for the remainder of the day, take in the sun and the relaxed environment.

Evening:

- Explore the lively nightlife of Kotor when you return in the evening. Go to the neighborhood pubs and bars that the locals frequent to see live music performances, DJ sets, and folk dances.

- Mix with locals and other tourists while sampling Montenegrin delicacies like rakija (fruit brandy), Nikšićko beer, or regional wines. Accept the friendliness and friendship that characterize Kotor's nightlife.

Day 3: Outdoor Adventures and Day Trip
Morning:

- Visit Perast, a quaint seaside village only a short drive from Kotor, for the day. Take a boat cruise to the neighboring islands, see the Church of Our Lady of the Rocks, and explore the historic center.
- Alternatively, go on an outdoor activity in the Bay of Kotor like paddleboarding or kayaking. Hideaway coves, sea caves, and rocky shorelines may be explored by renting equipment from a nearby outfitter.

In the afternoon:

- Savor fresh seafood and regional delicacies while taking in bay views at a beachside restaurant in Perast for lunch. Taste some grilled fish, seafood pasta, or black risotto with a crisp white wine.
- Proceed with your tour of Perast after lunch, or go back to Kotor for a leisurely afternoon. Wander idly along the seaside promenade, peruse local stores and boutiques, or schedule a massage or other wellness treatment at a nearby spa.

Evening:

- Visit a typical Kotor konoba or restaurant in the evening to savor robust Montenegrin food in a welcoming setting. Sample some lamb stew, grilled meats with ajvar (red pepper relish), or paul (bean soup).

- After supper, stroll around Kotor's ancient town in the evening and enjoy the atmosphere created by the lit streets and historical buildings. Have a late drink or a quiet talk while listening to live music at a neighborhood pub or café before turning in for the evening.

With this tour, you'll explore Kotor's ancient sites, undiscovered attractions, and outdoor experiences like a local and take in the rhythms and tastes of Montenegrin culture. Discover new things every day in this enchanted seaside resort, such as a relaxing stroll around the old town, picturesque treks, beachfront lunches, and exciting nights. Therefore, grab your spirit of adventure and explore Kotor's beauty and charm, where there are many opportunities to make lifelong memories.

Kotor foods and Dining options

Here is a thorough reference to the meals and eating alternatives that visitors and travelers may enjoy in Kotor, along with a list of suggested eateries:

Kotor's Local Cuisine & Dining Options:

1. Montenegro Cuisine:

Balkan staples, Adriatic seafood, and Mediterranean tastes all have an impact on Montenegrin cuisine. A selection of regional wines, cheeses, and olive oils go well with foods like grilled meats, fresh fish, robust stews, and flavorful pies.

Recommended Restaurants:

a. Konoba Scala Santa:

Trg od Salate, Old Town, Bay of Kotor, 85330, 85330, Montenegro
+382 67 393 458

This quaint taverna, situated in the ancient town of Kotor, specializes in serving traditional Montenegrin cuisine, including grilled meats, fish specialties, and housemade sweets. Savor substantial servings and cordial service in a casual setting.

b. Tanjga:

E65, Kotor, Montenegro

+382 69 863 836

Tanjga, a casual eating spot next to the main plaza, serves reasonably priced Balkan favorites including cevapi (grilled sausages), pljeskavica (grilled burgers), and mixed grill platters. Get takeout for a picnic by the bay or eat on the outside patio.

2. Restaurants Serving Seafood:

Kotor's coastline setting makes it home to a wide range of seafood eateries serving up fresh Adriatic Sea fish. Look for seafood risotto, grilled fish, octopus salad, and shellfish platters, all served with views of the sea and local wines.

Recommended Restaurants:

a. Galion

Šuranj bb, Kotor 85330, Montenegro
+382 67 263 420

Nestled on the seaside promenade, Galion has sweeping views of the bay along with a cuisine that changes seasonally and includes specialties of seafood. Savor seafood specialties such as lobster spaghetti, shrimp scampi, and grilled sea bass while taking in the sunset and sea wind.

b. Konoba Portun

168, Donji put, Dobrota, Montenegro
+382 68 086 101

Nestled in a historic building close to the port in Kotor, Konoba Portun offers inventive fish meals influenced by tastes from the Mediterranean and Adriatic. Savor regional specialties in a warm, welcoming atmosphere, such as grilled calamari, seafood stew, and black risotto with cuttlefish ink.

3. International Cuisine:

Kotor has a variety of foreign restaurants that provide food from all over the globe for visitors looking for a variety of eating alternatives. Seek for bistros in France, Asian fusion restaurants, Italian trattorias, and more.

Recommended Restaurants:
a. Galion Beach Club:

Šuranj bb, Kotor 85330, Montenegro
+382 67 263 420

Galion Beach Club delivers worldwide cuisine with a concentration on Mediterranean tastes in addition to seafood. Savor meals like spaghetti, grilled meats, and fresh salads while lounging on the beach.

b. Cesarica:

stari grad 375, Kotor 85330, Montenegro
+382 69 049 733

Nestled in the center of Kotor's historic district, Cesarica provides a flavor of Italy with its menu of antipasti platters, handmade pasta, and wood-fired pizzas. As you enjoy your meal, take in the atmosphere of the ancient surroundings with a crisp Aperol spritz or a bottle of Montenegrin wine.

4. Bakeries and Cafés:

Kotor is home to several bakeries and cafés where visitors may savor pastries, coffee, and other delicious delicacies all day long. In addition to worldwide favorites, look for native Montenegrin desserts including baklava, burek, and palatine (crepes).

Recommended Bakeries and Cafés:

a. Café del Mare:

34 Put I Bokeljske Brigade, Dobrota 85330, Montenegro
+382 67 279 189

Situated on the waterfront promenade, Cafe del Mare provides a variety of coffee drinks, teas, and cocktails along with breathtaking views of the bay. As you watch the boats pass, enjoy your drink with a piece of fresh cake or pastry.

b. Bakery Mamma Mia:

Unnamed Road, Kotor, Montenegro

Traditional Montenegrin pastries including burek, pita, and krone (doughnuts) are the specialty of this neighborhood bakery. Visit them for a quick breakfast or snack and sample their freshly baked delicacies, which are produced with ingredients that are obtained locally.

Travelers and visitors can pick from a variety of eating alternatives in Kotor, such as traditional Montenegrin food, specialties of fresh seafood, foreign cuisine, and sweet delights from bakeries and cafés.

This little seaside village has everything to sate your hunger, whether it's wood-fired pizza, freshly baked pastries, or grilled meats and seafood. Thus, throughout your vacation, take your time, sample Kotor's gastronomic offerings, and enjoy the tastes of Montenegro.

Comprehensive guide to Kotor's retail malls and shopping Centers:

1. Old Town Market in Kotor :

Gradske zine, Kotor, Montenegro

- The Old Town Market in Kotor is a hive of activity that provides a broad range of regional products, artisan crafts, trinkets, and fresh fruit. Situated in the center of the historic district, the market is an essential stop for tourists wishing to take in the lively ambiance and purchase one-of-a-kind souvenirs and presents.
- Peruse booths with jewelry produced by hand, pottery, textiles, and artwork created by regional artists. Taste classic Montenegrin treats like cheeses, olives, honey, and dried fruits, or purchase fresh vegetables, seasonings, and culinary herbs.
- Get to know regional producers and artists, discover customary techniques for crafting and cooking, and

take in the sights, sounds, and aromas of the market. Don't pass up the chance to negotiate and barter for the greatest prices on presents and mementos to bring home.

2. Kamelija Shopping Center:

Square Mata Petrovića, Kotor, Montenegro
+382 32 335 380

- One of Kotor's biggest shopping centers, Kamelija Shopping Center has a wide variety of retail establishments, shops, cafés, and entertainment venues all under one roof. Travelers and residents alike may enjoy a contemporary and pleasant shopping experience at this conveniently placed mall close to the old town.
- Look through a variety of specialist shops, foreign brands, and fashion boutiques that include apparel, accessories, shoes, makeup, gadgets, and more. Spend a leisurely evening seeing a movie at the theater or unwinding at one of the mall's eateries or cafés.

- Find distinctive presents and mementos to remember your trip to Kotor, or browse for the newest styles and designer brands in the comfort and convenience of air conditioning. Benefit from the mall's features, which include parking, free Wi-Fi, and accessibility for those with disabilities.

3. Trg Od Oruzja:

- Arms Square, also known as Trg od Oruzja, is a famous historic square in Kotor's old town that is well-known for its quaint architecture, antique stores, and artisan enterprises. Travelers looking for genuine Montenegrin crafts, gifts, and souvenirs often visit the area.
- Peruse booths and stores featuring handcrafted products manufactured by regional craftsmen, including woodcarvings, textiles, leather goods, and ceramics. Find one-of-a-kind mementos and unusual finds that perfectly encapsulate Montenegrin tradition and culture.
- Wander down Trg od Oruzja and take in the scenic surroundings and historic architecture that embodies the beauty of Kotor's old town. Talk to retailers and artists, discover their craft customs, and bring home a treasured piece of Montenegrin workmanship.

4. Green Market:

CQFC+H5G, E65, Kotor 85330, Montenegro

- The Green Market, also known as Pijaca, is a colorful outdoor market that sells a variety of fresh produce, herbs, fruits, and local delicacies. It is situated close to Kotor's old town. The market, which is open every day, is a popular destination for both residents and tourists to purchase in-season vegetables and delectable foods.
- Stroll through rows of booths filled with vibrant fruits and vegetables, savory herbs and spices, freshly produced pastries and cheeses, and cured meats and bread. Try some regional specialties like

rakija (fruit brandy), ajvar (red pepper relish), and prosciutto. You may also talk to sellers about their goods and cooking techniques.

- Wander around the Green Market and take in the sights, sounds, and aromas of a classic Balkan market while chatting with farmers and producers and tasting Montenegro's cuisine. Stock up on supplies for a picnic or to cook at your lodging and enjoy the quality and freshness of locally produced cuisine.

5. Voli Supermarket:

21. Novembra, Tivat 85320, Montenegro
+382 67 624 026

- Voli Supermarket is a well-known grocery store chain in Montenegro that provides a large selection of food items, home goods, cosmetics, and other stuff. Travelers and residents alike may enjoy easy shopping choices at the several Voli shops located around Kotor.

- Peruse aisles filled with exotic food items, dairy goods, meats, fresh fruit, and pantry necessities. Get drinks, food, and picnic materials for your explorations of Kotor, or do a grocery run while you're here.
- Take advantage of the contemporary convenience of a well-stocked supermarket with affordable pricing and attentive service. For extra convenience, Voli Supermarket now provides internet shopping, reward programs, and self-checkout choices.

6. TQ Plaza:

85310, 53 Mediteranska, Budva, Montenegro
+382 68 855 855

- In the center of Kotor, TQ Plaza is a mixed-use complex that has upscale residences, cafés, restaurants, and retail stores. Along with a variety of high-end boutiques, designer shops, and global brands, the complex offers food and entertainment alternatives.
- Look through stores selling footwear, accessories, and apparel from well-known brands and designers. Explore upscale jewelry, cosmetics, and watches, or treat yourself to exquisite dining and good wines in the plaza's cafés and restaurants.
- Shop for high-end clothing, accessories, and lifestyle goods in a chic and contemporary environment at TQ Plaza, where you can get a taste of luxury and refinement. Take in expansive views of the harbor and old town from the outdoor terraces of the plaza, or unwind in the internal atrium surrounded by shops and restaurants.

As a traveler, you can enjoy a wide range of shopping experiences in Kotor, from contemporary malls and boutiques to traditional marketplaces and artisan workshops. This picturesque seaside town has plenty to offer everyone's preferences and interests, whether they are looking for fresh fruit, local specialties, handcrafted crafts, or the newest fashions. Take your time, stroll around Kotor's marketplaces and retail areas, and look for the hidden gems and distinctive mementos that lie in wait for you while you're there.

Kotor Festivals and Events

1. Kotor Carnival:
Period of the Year: February
Held in the weeks before Lent, the Kotor Carnival, also called the Pustovanje, is a vivacious event. The carnival, which dates back centuries, is known for its spectacular costumes, vibrant parades, street acts, music, and dancing.
Take in the magnificent masks and costumes worn by residents and tourists as they march through Kotor's ancient town, complete with music and dance. Take in the joyous ambiance, indulge in classic carnival fare like fritule (fried dough balls), and take part in events like mask-making classes and masquerade balls.
Tips: To truly enjoy the festivities, arrive early to gain a good viewing place along the parade route. Also, don't forget to dress in character for the carnival. Throughout the carnival season, keep a look out for unique activities and performances that are planned.
2. International Fashion Festival:
Period of the Year: June

The International Fashion Festival, held in Kotor, is a distinguished occasion that presents the newest styles and creations from global fashion designers. The festival features runway presentations, fashion exhibits, seminars, and networking opportunities for industry experts and fashion aficionados, all of which are held in picturesque locations around the city.

See opulent runway presentations with upcoming designers from Montenegro and beyond, as well as couture and ready-to-wear collections. Visit fashion shows that include cutting-edge apparel, accessories, and photography, and participate in panel discussions and seminars on sustainability and business trends.

Tips: To guarantee a good seat at runway shows and special events, get tickets in advance. Also, come early. At networking events and after-parties, dress to impress and be ready to interact with designers, models, and fashion influencers.

3. KotorArt International Festival:

Period of the Year : July–August

The KotorArt International Festival honors music, dance, theater, visual arts, and cinema as multidimensional forms of art. The festival, which takes place in historic locations throughout Kotor, offers educational programs, seminars, exhibits, and performances for audiences of all ages.

Take in cinema screenings, ballet performances, theater shows, art installations, and concerts by well-known performers in locations including squares, cathedrals, and historic buildings. Take part in master courses and workshops conducted by artists and performers, and connect with the local artistic community by attending exhibits and interactive events.

Tips: For a schedule of activities and performances, see the festival program and make plans for your stay. To experience the lively atmosphere of the festival, get tickets in advance for popular shows and performances, and think about going to free outdoor concerts and activities.

4. Boka Night:

Period of the Year : August

Boka Night is a customary festivity observed in Kotor to pay tribute to the city's maritime past and patron saint, Saint Tryphon. The celebration culminates in a joyous mood throughout the city and includes religious processions, boat parades, fireworks, live music, and cultural events.

Take in the bay's vibrant parade of boats, complete with lights and flags, as they pass by, backed by cheering spectators and music. Come enjoy live music, dancing, and traditional Montenegrin cuisine and beverages from food sellers in Kotor's streets alongside residents and tourists.

Tips: Be ready for large crowds and exciting festivities, and arrive early to guarantee a good viewing place for the boat procession and fireworks show. Don casual attire and footwear appropriate for outdoor events, and don't forget to indulge in regional delicacies like grilled fish, shellfish, and rakija (fruit brandy).

5. Kotor International Camellia Festival:

Period of the Year : April

The Kotor International Camellia Festival honors the beauty of camellias via artistic exhibits, guided garden tours, and cultural activities. The event presents the city's ancient gardens and green areas as well as Kotor's rich horticultural legacy.

Wander around Kotor's parks and gardens, which are decked out in a variety of hues and species of camellia blossoms. Attend talks and guided tours on the history, significance, and cultivation of camellias. You may also take part in gardening and floral design workshops.

Tips: Make sure you organize your visit by looking up the schedule of activities, exhibits, and garden tours in the festival program. Seize the chance to see Kotor's picturesque settings and pick the brains of knowledgeable and passionate gardeners.

6. KotorArt Don Branko's Music:

Period of the Year: September

Held in honor of Don Branko Sbutega, a significant person in Kotor's cultural history, KotorArt Don Branko's Music Days is a well-known classical music event. World-class performers and groups will be giving masterclasses, concerts, recitals, and chamber music performances throughout the festival.

Take in concerts by renowned orchestras and performers throughout the world in old buildings including squares, cathedrals, and palaces. Take in the allure of classical music in Kotor's enchanting environs while taking part in seminars and talks on music education and enjoyment.

Tips: To guarantee a good seat for concerts and recitals, get your tickets in advance and come early. Benefit from the educational events and networking opportunities offered by the festival for professionals, students, and music enthusiasts.

7. Kotor Festival of Theatre for Children:

Period of the Year: October

The Kotor Festival of Theatre for Children is a family-friendly celebration of the performing arts that includes interactive workshops, storytelling, puppetry, and theatrical shows. The festival wants to encourage young audiences and their families to be imaginative, and creative, and to share cultures.

Take in performances at various locations across Kotor by regional and international theater groups, puppeteers, and storytellers. Take part in interactive workshops and events that inspire kids to learn about the performing arts, dance, and storytelling.

Tips: Refer to the festival program to see what events, seminars, and performances are appropriate for various age groups. When visiting Kotor, take the entire family and immerse yourself in the enchanted realm of tale and theater.

Kotor has several festivals and events all year long that highlight the city's rich cultural history, creative talent, and a thriving sense of community. There's always something going on in Kotor to captivate and excite visitors of all stripes, from vibrant carnivals and fashion shows to international art festivals and customary festivities. Thus, be sure to schedule your vacation appropriately, take part in the celebrations, and make treasured memories while visiting this charming seaside town.

Navigating Kotor Nightlife: Bars, Clubs, and Entertainment Venues

Here is a comprehensive guide to Kotor's nightlife, which includes bars, clubs, and entertainment venues:

1. Club Maximus:

CQG9+7H8, Kotor, Montenegro
+382 67 217 101

Situated in the center of Kotor's old town, club Maximus is one of the city's biggest and most well-liked nightlife destinations. The club has many levels, each with a distinct vibe and selection of pop, house, and electronic music.

Unwind in one of the club's VIP rooms with bottle service and other amenities, or dance the night away on the main dance floor to the sounds of renowned DJs and live acts. Savor important occasions, themed evenings, and visits from foreign performers.

Advice: To prevent lengthy lines, visit early and check the club's calendar for forthcoming events and performances. There is a stringent dress code at Maximus Club, so come dressed to impress. The night will be filled with energy and a dynamic environment.

2. Old Winery

483 Zanatska, Kotor, Montenegro
+382 69 397 390

The Old Winery is a chic wine bar in Kotor's old town that offers a classy but laid-back setting for mingling and wine connoisseurs. It is housed in a historic structure. Together with specialty drinks and gourmet nibbles, the bar offers a broad wine selection that includes both domestic and foreign varieties.

Enjoy excellent wines by the glass or bottle, carefully chosen by staff members who are experienced and willing to suggest combinations. Take in live music, poetry readings, or art exhibits while savoring regional cheeses, charcuterie, and tapas-style cuisine.

Advice: Take advantage of the bar's happy hour offers and wine sampling events, and make reservations in advance for table dining, particularly during busy times. Indulge in the rustic-chic ambiance within or take in views of the sea and old town from the outside patio.

3. Culture Club Tarantino:

Bokeška br. 6, Montenegro
+382 67 055 333

Near Kotor's main square, Culture Club Tarantino is a trendy and eccentric club that's well-known for its unique décor, retro ambiance, and wide range of musical tastes. The pub draws a diverse clientele of visitors and residents, fostering an inclusive environment.

Enjoy custom shots, handmade cocktails, and local beers while exploring the eccentric atmosphere of the pub, which is decorated with movie posters, old furniture, and unusual artwork. Dance to a wide variety of musical selections provided by resident DJs and special guests, including rock, indie, funk, and techno.

Advice: Be sure to check the bar's social media accounts for information on forthcoming events, theme nights, and live music. You may also come early to guarantee a seat on the outside terrace or dance floor. Take advantage of the chance to try the bar's specialty drinks and inventive drink specials.

4. Gradska Kafana:

31 Njegoševa, Herceg - Novi, Montenegro
+382 31 321 066

In the center of Kotor's ancient town, Gradska Kafana is a classic pub that provides genuine Montenegrin hospitality in a relaxed setting. The tavern is a favored hangout for both residents and tourists since it hosts live music, folk performances, and karaoke nights.

Savor delicious seafood delicacies, grilled meats, and Montenegrin cuisine accompanied by regional wines, beers, and spirits. Attend live music events featuring local bands and performers, or participate in entertaining sing-alongs and karaoke sessions.

Advice: To guarantee a table near the stage, make reservations well in advance, particularly on weekends and during the busiest travel times. You should also come early. Welcome to Gradska Kafana, where you may socialize with the locals, sing, dance, and meet new people long into the night.

Kotor provides visitors and tourists with a lively and diversified nightlife scene, whether they want to dance the night away at a busy nightclub, drink great wines in a secluded wine bar, or experience the local way of life at a traditional tavern. Plan your evening activities appropriately, check out the pubs, clubs, and entertainment areas in the city, and then take in Kotor's vibrant nightlife.

.

Sustainable Travel in Kotor: Responsible Tourism Practices

In Kotor, sustainable travel entails using ethical tourism techniques to reduce adverse effects on the environment, assist local populations, and protect the area's cultural legacy. This is a guide to eco-friendly travel methods in Kotor:

1. Select Eco-Friendly Lodging:

- Select lodging options such as eco-lodges, guesthouses, and hotels that emphasize sustainable practices including water conservation, trash reduction, and energy efficiency.
- Seek lodging that has earned certification from reputable eco-labels or get involved in environmentally friendly activities like organic gardening and recycling.

2. Diminish Your Carbon Imprint:

- To lessen your dependence on carbon-emitting automobiles, explore Kotor and the nearby regions by walking, biking, or using public transit wherever feasible.
- Choose eco-friendly modes of transportation like car-sharing or electric taxis to offset your travel

emissions. You may also support carbon offset programs.

3. Encourage regional companies:

- Consume food from neighboring farms and markets at locally owned eateries to support the community's economy and cut down on food miles.
- Buy trinkets and handicrafts from regional cooperatives and artists to support residents' livelihoods and the preservation of traditional crafts.

4. Show Consideration for the Environment:

- When hiking or visiting natural areas, stick to authorized routes and walkways to prevent harm to delicate ecosystems and animal habitats.
- Recycle and utilize designated trash cans to properly dispose of garbage; avoid single-use plastics and littering.

5. Get Knowledge of the History and Culture:

- Learn about the history, customs, and traditions of Kotor and its people by interacting with local guides and visiting cultural heritage sites.
- Ask permission before taking pictures or taking part in ceremonies at holy locations, monuments, and cultural customs.

6. Preserve Energy and Water:

- Reduce the amount of water you use by reusing towels, taking shorter showers, and reporting any leaks or waste in your lodging.
- When not in use, switch off the lights, air conditioning, and electronics. You may also pick energy-efficient lodging and transportation.

7. Do Not Remain Behind:

- Preserve natural environments by not damaging flora or fauna and by taking any trash or litter with you when you leave.
- Refrain from plucking plants or flowers, remain on designated pathways, and don't disturb animals to lessen your influence on delicate ecosystems.

You can help ensure that future generations may continue to enjoy this enchanted place by adopting sustainable travel habits while visiting Kotor. This will help preserve the city's natural beauty, cultural legacy, and communal well-being.

Have a great Trip

Printed in Great Britain
by Amazon